THE UNOPENED DOOR

THE UNOPENED DOOR:

Christianity Facing the Occult

RON MATTHIES

AUGSBURG PUBLISHING HOUSE
Minneapolis, Minnesota

NEWBOOKS

THE UNOPENED DOOR

Manufactured in the United States of America

CONTENTS

ON THE THRESHOLD

I am at a party, a gaggle of fine people talk wittingly of theology, church organization, recent literature. Then, a neat-haired, yellow-dressed woman says to me, "Well, I don't know. I see both sides. I just can't decide."

"A typical Gemini," I say. The room silences.

"How did you know?" she says.

I shrug — a characteristic occult gesture. She confesses that she is a Gemini (born May 21-June 21). Soon, I am listing the characteristics of her sign: Quick minded. Intellectual. Lovers of experience. Find it difficult to choose between alternatives.

She says, "I'm interested, but I've always felt guilty about astrology. I worry it's sinful or anti-Christian."

I could quote poets, presidents, reformers who believed in astrology, but I say, "Is it sinful to know yourself better? Don't you think a God who cares for his people might leave some clues about our character? I like to keep my mind open to all possibilities and judge later."

I would like to say more. I would like to tell her that astrology is not fatalistic, that our inclinations, not our destinies are written in the stars. But I can say little more because the crowd has assembled. Each in turn asks, "What am I?" They nod in turn as I explain the age-old attributes of their sun signs. Or, they scoff and say, "Nonsense! I'm not like that at all." So the evening spins away and I remain the center of attention — an Aries doesn't mind.

I am not telling you of a minor party in my life as the

beginning of an autobiography, but because I feel many Christians who secretly turn to the more than 2000 astrological columns in the newspapers or who buy the proliferation of magazines on the occult feel very guilty and slightly sinful just as my yellow Geminian lady did. I think this attitude is understandable, but inaccurate.

Occult Economics

The other thing revealed by my experience at the party was a swelling tidal wave of interest in the occult. This interest is not confined to quiet gatherings. Rather, it is so strong that its economic star is in the sky. Look around. You'll find zodiac posters, cookbooks, cat horoscopes, plastic mugs in grocery stores, paper plates, ads saying, "The perfect rug for a Scorpio." A popular song, "The Age of Aquarius," murmurs, "When the moon is in its seventh house/and Jupiter aligns with Mars. . . ." One could furnish a home, eat his meals, sleep, drink, and carry out all his functions with a zodiacal symbol in every proper place. This economic gobbling is the harmless, perhaps frivolous side of the occult. Although I do wonder whether the money spent on Sagittarian paper plates could not have been better used for psychological research. Alas, the psychologist is probably working on consumer attitudes anyhow.

The Darker Side

Unfortunately the occult has not just proliferated paper plates, but also the demonic:

• Sirhan Sirhan when given a choice of books after his imprisonment asked for *The Secret Doctrine* by Madame Blavatsky. This turn-of-the-century occultist and founder of the

Theosophists would have spiralled in mid-incarnation at this usage of her book and would have been appalled by Kennedy's murder.

• Sandor de La Vey heads the Church of Satan where the Devil is worshiped, Christian services parodied, and ritual orgies held.

• *Rosemary's Baby*, popular novel and movie, produced an occult child from woman and the Devil in a literary celebration of erotostupidity.

• March, 1970, *Esquire* devoted to evil, reports a witch, self-named Leda, trying to produce a child with a little help from a swan.

• The Tate murders and Manson trial reek of hypnosis, ritual markings, and Manson himself as the underground hero of a whole new cult.

I find the last two particularly disturbing, for, while the occult has often wed with drugs, it has always been an unhappy marriage. And, I think Leda and Manson are victims not of the occult but of the drugs. The drugs and cornucopia of psychedelics reveal that the cosmos is not the logical orderly pattern we learned; this may incline towards the occult which explains mystically not mechanistically. Yet this sharing of parts does not mean and should not mean the occult is allied with drugs. It is opposed to it.

But it is exactly because of these misunderstandings, because many Christians feel guilt over interest in astrology or other occult arts, and because of the swelling interest, good and bad, that a book on the occult is helpful and necessary to understand this handmaiden of the youthquake, to understand these ancient arts themselves, and even to understand yourself.

1 KNOCKING AT THE DOOR

The occult conjures strange fancies and dim images of casting spells, hexing, star gazing, and staring into crystal balls. But these are images of black or slack magic. The word *occult* merely means what is hidden or unknown. It could encompass anything from the creation of the world to the Van Allen belt. Early Christianity shows the division between the public ritual and the private communion (occult or hidden) for the baptized knowers of the resurrected Christ.

Who Is an Occultist?

To become a "member" of the esoteric in any branch of the occult involves either knowledge and/or initiation. And it is with the emphasis on knowledge or wisdom that we find a major cleavage between Christianity and branches on the tree of the occult. The occult is based on the perfectability of man through wisdom and right action; Christianity insists on the corruptibility of man and salvation through faith. So, while many of the ideas and beliefs of the occult are similar to Christianity, they cannot join over a common altar.

Even though they cannot share an altar, Christians need not be closed to the occult. A religion which accepts the countless miracles of the Bible, beautiful and profound, cannot deny the supernatural. A religion based on figures who could plumb the innermost depths of man and interpret the dreams of Pharaoh or a king of Babylon should not deny the realm of the psychic. Even the many biblical warnings against sorcerers, witches, and magicians are ones both a good occultist and a Christian would heed. All biblical warnings from the Witch of Endor to Simon Magus are against selfish desire for knowledge, fatalistic magic, or presuming the power of God himself.

Since the world of the occult clings to religion and is part of a religious system, its beliefs must be defined. However, the task is as impossible as uniting Lutheranism and Islam, because the basic similarities in all branches of the occult are rarely recognized, and few practicing occultists organize. Occultism, then, is based more on common recognitions than on common beliefs. Most men recognize something larger than themselves, which directs, creates, and gives order to our world. Most realize that people are both good and evil, and they see a rhythm to life. Finally, most hope there is something beyond, a means of understanding the order, and a method of being at one with this supreme being. These are common recognitions of all great religions.

God Is a Circle

If you take a pen and draw a circle, you may have the first symbolic representation of God. A circle is continuous, without beginning or end. It can hold all or be completely empty. While this may be a valid picture of God, it doesn't satisfy our longing to know what he is like. Many Christians believe that God is all-knowing, all-powerful, all-seeing, Lord, King, Savior. Occultists will not usually go so far. Most would feel more comfortable with the sayings of the Chinese sage, Lao Tzu, and his description of Tao, as close to God as his religion comes:

The Tao that can be expressed is not eternal Tao;
The name that can be defined is not the unchanging name.

Although we could skip down rows of epochs and eras to the source of occultism's deity in moon worship, cow worship, sun worship, fertility worship, even self worship, we always reach the No Exit sign: "The God that can be expressed is not eternal God." Gazing at our circle is not enough. From it, we can only perceive that there is a One, a supreme being who orders this rag and bone shop of the world. We can conjecture that everything in life proceeds from the One, that the wish of every person is to know the will of the One, and that the goal of all is to return to the One.

The Dotted Circle

Our indescribable One created. This is obvious. I am here. You are here.

If we represent creation by a dot in the middle of the circle, we have a symbol of this creation. The circle is now a container for something. In astrology this dotted circle is the sign of the sun and represents man. Man is in the direct center of the One's creation. Of ultimate importance to the occultist, this means that man is *part* of the one, not a distinctly separate being as in Christianity. At best, the occultist accepts this oneness with humility. At worst, some feel that as part of God they can become God and mold the universe to their liking. Yet this denial of God's grace lifting man separates Christianity from occultism.

How the One theoretically created is the basis of much occultism. Many say it was through language. The sacred syllable Om of Hinduism, indeed the entire Sanskrit language, is sacred because it was the means of creation. Jewish mysticism claims creation through the 22 sacred letters of the Hebrew alphabet.

We have in creation through language the seedlings of numerology, the Tarot, and aspects of astrology.

Dividing the Circle

Man beholds the creation of the One. And he knows beneath the scrap and joggles and jolts there must be a pattern. The pattern is hard to find. We have birth and green fields and daisies and love and happiness, but we also have death and snowy pastures and hemlock and sadness. It seems for everything good, the balance of evil tags along its drooping tail. At least a pattern begins. There is a rhythm in the seasons, a pulse to life and death, a balance between joy and sorrow.

For most of mankind, excluding Christianity, there is a line drawn through our circle. One half is positive or good; the other, negative or evil. This basic dualism underlies most of the occult which teaches that everything exists because of its opposite — light because of darkness, summer because of winter, life because of death. Once this dualism is accepted, it becomes the task of man to reconcile the opposites. Again, it is the Chinese who best reflect this dualism; they saw not just an orderly pattern, but that all forces of nature were in conflict. From this fact they realized that harmony must be achieved through a balance of positive and negative forces which are in constant interaction. As the years passed, they detected these forces in all of nature and pictured it as shown on the opposite page.

Half the circle is *yang,* all that is positive, masculine, active, productive, hot, dry, bright, and assertive. *Yin* is negative, female, passive, receptive, cool, moist, shadowy, and yielding. Philosophy gives way to the occult in a book called the *I Ching* or Book of Changes, which shows all possible combinations of *yang-yin,* the means of balancing the forces, and the fortune that

will result from each. Through a fairly simple process, the person wishing to know divine will casts coins or sticks, which combine in one of 64 hexagrams. These six-line figures, combinations of *yang-yin,* supposedly show all the possibilities of life in ever-changing nature. While the purpose is divination, much of the advice seems cryptic to the Western mind. For example, suppose Hexagram 48 is cast. It says: "Looking at Ching, we think of how a town may be changed, while its well undergoes no change. The water of the well never disappears and never receives increase, and those who come and those who go can draw and enjoy the benefit. If the drawing have nearly been accomplished, but, before the rope is broken, this is evil." Delphic advice, but it does serve well to show a dynamic nature consisting of the forever playing dualities.

Whirling Round the Circle

That Eastern religions and most of the occult do not worship evil is shown by the basic beliefs of *karma* and reincarnation. Reincarnation means the existence of the soul through many lifetimes to attain perfection. This possibility of perfection again separates Christianity and the occult, for forgiveness, grace, and atonement have no place in the world of reincarnation. "As a man sows, so shall he reap" is the law of *karma* and *karma* is what links incarnations. A good life should lead to a better one and ultimately to perfection and absorption back into the One; conversely, a bad life leads to a worse one in the future. Getting a "bad karma" has become a popular expression for descending in one's next life or of feeling the effects from a previous bad incarnation. Far from being malevolent, karmic law is infinitely patient. It gives man countless lifetimes to perfect himself. While the soul or self is on the "other side" or between incarnations, man, still conscious of his past life, reflects on the good and bad deeds committed, then chooses his next life and how he will live it to pay the karmic debts accrued. And the ultimate goal— a return to the One—is worthy enough reward for a believer.

Many aspects of reincarnation contain unanswerable questions and conflicting opinions. What is passed from life to life? The soul? Probably so, but not a passing on of personality. How do we know reincarnation occurs? We don't. With birth into a new body, we forget the past. Memory is denied in reincarnation. But much recent investigation under hypnosis points to previous existences.

Contrary to popular debunking, very few claim to have been Napoleon, Jesus, or Queen Victoria. Common lives of common men have been traced. A famous and documented case occurred in the 1940s to an Indian girl, Shanti Devi. Born in Delhi, at a very early age she began talking of her husband, Kedar Nath, and her home, Madura, hundreds of miles away. She said her name was Lugdi. Although a Hindu, she knew much about Islam. She even told of a sum of money hidden under a floorboard before she died. After much discussion, her parents took her to Madura. She found her home, recognized Kedar Nath, lifted the proper floorboard, but Kedar Nath admitted to taking the money after Lugdi died. Next door in a crowd of 50, she embraced a woman; it was her mother. Coincidence?

How long are we on the "other side"? Occultists and researchers disagree. One year to 400 is accepted. The nature of the other side is supposedly peaceful, a place for questioning, a place of communication with others as Bishop Pike's *The Other Side* indicates. It should not be confused with the ultimate goal, at-one-ness, which like the One cannot be described.

Reincarnation seems inconsistent with grace and forgiveness, the at-one-ment received through Christ.

Full Circle — Practices

As I said, initiation and knowledge or wisdom are necessary to the occultist. Initiation means a passing through and an entrance into something—the ultimate goal, at-one-ness. It may be as fast as a ritual of Bacchus or as slow as the circle of reincarnation. No matter what the speed, necessary knowledge is assumed.

And all of the basic tools of the occult's wisdom grow out of a desire to enter into the Oneness. The nature of this wisdom's discovery is lost in history. A likely means of achieving wisdom is to assume that God's ultimate product — man — is *like* God. So God is man writ large; man is God writ small. Similarly, the actions of the heavens lead to another *like*. God is above. Man is below. What occurs below, must be a reflection of divine action above. This is the root of astrology. The dualistic world of God means opposites must be reconciled. The obvious means is to imitate divine action. This is the source of magic.

These analogies may lead to shortcut initiations. One shortcut initiation is to concentrate on one of the tools of wisdom, such as astrology, to know divine will, get quick answers, and leap into the One. Worse yet, the analogy of man to God can lead the occultist to think he can control and master all of the elements and become God himself. Here is black magic. Finally, a seeker might concentrate on one pole of life—the evil—and with infinite discipline become a Satanist. The failing of all shortcuts is that they are self-ish. The desire is to increase the power of the self, not to unite with the One.

The true seeker, realizing initiation may take many lifetimes, accepts all of the world, including his own insignificance, and forgets the self. Once the self is forgotten, man is free in his search for wisdom. This quest is not for knowledge based on shortcut at-one-ness, but for wisdom, wisdom that unites and integrates all of life. The path is long and arduous. It requires great discipline as shown in Chapter 3. Within the initiation path are the elements of all doors to the one: Humility. Courage. Symbolic death. Discipline. Knowledge of the tools. The wisdom of the ages. This is the pattern of all initiations including Christian baptism—and acceptance into a witches' coven.

A few people are granted without shoddy magic or questionable tools, great gifts that make the long and arduous initiation into the psychic or mysterious unnecessary. I cannot explain why psychics such as Cayce or Garrett (Chapter 6) exist, why they know the future. They do. To some degree psychic ability is necessary for any initiation, but it remains amazing that some are granted it without a slow, disciplined way. Yet psychology finds it harder and harder to deny that some possess Extrasensory Perception (ESP) which may be just heightened sensitivity to the world or divine gift. It is as difficult to deny that some see the future, can move objects by their will and contact spirits on the other side; yet science can find no explanation. Many occultists would say they are "old souls" almost perfected through reincarnations who are so close to the One that the discipline, the knowledge of the tools, the slow climb, are lost in an easy and deserved communication with the One.

An Occult Church?

How many occultists know the beliefs I have spun or accept them is impossible to guess. Yet each branching of the occult springs from the sources of belief I have mentioned. Some may represent only one aspect of the beliefs. Others may accept many, but disagree on such a point as dualism. Some might accept all. Each is a branch of the disciplined way.

So, there is no First Church of the Occult. Rather, there is a system of beliefs *underlying* the occult, but not always manifested in practice. There are some aspects of the occult which create religion such as dualism and Taoism. But there is not now, has not been, and probably never will be a unified occult movement.

2 THE GOLDEN KEY:

ASTROLOGY

Lurching on the train to Minneapolis for Christmas, I heard over the white doilies, "I mean Mussolini and Napoleon were double Leos, too." Later, "His eyes like hynotize you. He has five planets in Scorpio, like Manson." By the end of the ride, the sweet young thing had asked me to chart her horoscope since it is so difficult (which it is not) and explain her moon in Sagittarius because "Sags are so freaky" (which they are not). A believer.

I am at a faculty party. We've discussed women's lib, college politics, inflation and . . . "I don't believe in this occult stuff you're doing, Ron. But it sounds interesting. Explain it."

I say, "What aspect?"

"All of it." My moan is inward, my explanation terse, and it ignores two snorting scientists on the fringes of the room. "Well, I still don't believe, but could you do my horoscope? What do we have to do? Turn off the lights? Join hands? Sit in a circle?" When I explain that I need books, paper, and mathematical calculations, we return to campus politics. No ghosties or ghoulies, just a yawn and mathematical calculations. Nonbelievers.

Despite ignorance or snorts, the interest in astrology is astounding. A recent poll indicates 90% of the American populace knew their sun sign, while only 65% knew the name of their senator, and I will not tell the embarrassing figure for those who knew the books of the Bible.

Slop Astrology

The interest burgeons in an age anxious for quick answers, slick answers, answers they can find in 1200 daily astro-advice columns. Maybe with a conjectural individual we can trace how interest buds and blooms. One day on the bus after reading the cartoons and want ads, our novice, Mr. Gemini, notices a column called "Star Tips." He scans down, finds his birthday. "Aha! May 23. I'm a Gemini." Advice for the day:

Star Tips by Ra Matt

ARIES (March 21-April 19) Work with groups as result of a trip. Do not try to impress others with your superiority.

TAURUS (April 20-May 21) Something of interest in social or gossip columns. Do not use information to hurt others through bellowing it like a bull.

GEMINI (May 22-June 21) Crawl out from behind your work worry and face the world as it is. Be cheerful.

This column contradicts two basic precepts of reputable astrology: *Individuality* (the column lumps everyone into 12 neat categories) and *free will* (for the day seems predestined for all). Yet suppose that Mr. Gemini is on the bus because he's looking for a job and is rather depressed. Reread his advice. So, although millions of others found nothing in "Star Tips," Mr. Gemini has matched circumstances and column. He is ready for Stage Two.

Pop Astrology

Rush out and by the latest edition of *Astroprops*. Here is a magazine devoted solely to astrology. Surely, more reputable. So, Mr. Gemini buys and reads the characteristics of the 12 signs:

ARIES (March 21-April 19). Our fiery ram leads the flock. He is the pioneer of the zodiac with a flaming will and a need to compete with anyone, using his good intellect to batter his way through all obstacles. Don't confine him, or his bad temper will flare and you'll see the aggressive, headstrong face of Aries. Console yourself with being one of his many friends. Watch out that he doesn't put too many irons in the fire, for he often doesn't finish what he starts, then needs underlings and can be terribly bossy. Some of his starmates include: Eugene McCarthy, Robert Frost, Haydn, Marlon Brando, Thomas Jefferson, Aretha Franklin, Diana Ross.

TAURUS (April 20-May 20). You can rely on the steady, plodding patient Tarus native. He is self-reliant and strong. Always practical, he loves nature and has a green thumb. Physical love is important to him as is accumulating money and what it will buy. But don't try to break his routine, he doesn't like changes. If satisfied with his surroundings he'll be endlessly faithful. He may have a tough hide, but underneath he's vulnerable. Although slow to anger, don't wave the red flag, for Taurus can be a terrible enemy just as he can be a life long friend. Taureans are good workers and obedient followers. Starmates: Shakespeare, Ulysses S. Grant, James Audubon, Harry Truman, Sigmund Freud, Barbra Streisand, and Elizabeth II.

GEMINI (May 21-June 21). This airy, mercurial sign has a dual personality. For example, he may wear mod clothes one day and a button-down collar and suit the next. Gemini is versatile, quick, mentally alert, but may be unable to commit himself to one person or one field of activity. Manic ups and depressive downs cause nervous action, and he may wear himself and others out. With his natural feeling for words and language, he has a fondness for learning if he can concentrate long enough to succeed at anything. Watch out for his decisions. He often has a changing viewpoint without any real convictions. Starmates: John Wayne, Hubert Humphrey, John F. Kennedy, Norman Vincent Peale, Marilyn Monroe, Judy Garland, John Wesley, Paul McCartney.

CANCER (June 22-July 22). The Moonchild is highly sensitive and emotional. He is strongly possessive and very affectionate to his family, sometimes tied to parents or his children. He may be moody and clinging, but he is also sympathetic and self-sacrificing. His intuition often makes him cautious and highly survival-conscious. He is at his best in vocations that protect and help others, but he wants his own ideas executed in his way. Never ridicule him, it brings out his worst—touchiness. Be happy with his best—persistence. Starmates: Don Drysdale, Franz Kafka, Ringo Starr, Nelson Rockefeller, Ingmar Bergman, Rembrandt, Art Linkletter, Mary Baker Eddy, and Barbara Stanwyck.

LEO (July 23-August 22). He is the king of our twelve, self-assured, authoritative, magnanimous, warm, and generous. He likes the limelight but will work hard for it and is practical. While he tends to dramatize everything and loves to impress others, he stands for every admirable cause. A natural joiner, he seeks lively people. His strong determination to rise may let his emotions control his intellect. But with his large majestic ideas, courage, strong physique, he seldom falls prey to his worst traits of overreaching for his goal and being conceited. Starmates: Ernest Hemingway, Henry VIII, James Baldwin, Andy Warhol, Alfred Hitchcock, Napoleon, Mussolini, Jackie Onassis, Ingrid Bergman, and Lucille Ball.

VIRGO (August 23-September 22). Virgo is a natural helper — humble, loyal, self-sacrificing. Rest easy if you give Virgo a job. He is happy as second in command. While compassionate, he may be overly critical. Virgo is a walking encyclopedia of facts, not theories, and never rests until the results are reached. With great objectivity, Virgo's best quality is an analytic mind, but he can be too critical and judge others too severely. Starmates: Leonard Bernstein, LBJ, Elizabeth I (the virgin queen), D. H. Lawrence, Anne Bancroft, Sophia Loren, Lauren Bacall, and Greta Garbo.

LIBRA (September 23-October 23). Libra is the weigher who loves peace, harmony, and justice. Seeking balance, he will look at both sides of everything. This makes for a good administrator. Librans love travel and varied experiences. They also like to learn and share with the friends they seek so avidly. Their love of beauty makes them attractive and graceful people; their easy temper makes them a joy to be around. But they may be overly fond of flattery and can be indecisive. Their love of experience can make them try too many things. But above all they appreciate, create, and equalize. Starmates: F. Scott Fitzgerald, William Faulkner, T. S. Eliot, Euripides, Julie Andrews, Emily Post, John Lennon, Eleanor Roosevelt, Eisenhower, Mahatma Gandhi, and Arthur Miller.

SCORPIO (October 24-November 23). This is the most misunderstood of all signs. It is the sign of extremes—perfect faithfulness or flagrant self-indulgence. Scorpios seem wholly self-sufficient and secretive yet are reliable and responsible. Scorpios are so complex no one seems to know them; their aloof air of superiority may result from their innately discerning nature. They are good fighters and fastidious in selection of friends, who must be intelligent and successful. This is the most passionate sign of all with great magnetism, but they may be suspicious and jealous. It is the worst sign to have for an enemy. Starmates: Picasso, Theodore Roosevelt, Richard Burton, Dostoievsky, Princess Grace, St. Augustine, and Robert Kennedy.

SAGITTARIUS (November 23-December 21). This most youthful of signs is the sportsman and playboy. A born enthusiast, he often inspires others. He is intuitive, even prophetic. It is the home of the promoter, visionary, and adventurer. So friendly, the Sagittarian will be the most popular person in any circle. A born traveler, he likes long or short trips. He is idealistic, philosophic, adaptable, and loyal. His worst trait is that he may become the foot-loose wanderer. Starmates: Winston Churchill, Mary Martin, Walt Disney, Emily Dickenson, Nostradamus, and Beethoven.

CAPRICORN (December 22-January 19). The most ambitious sign, he will work hard and is a born administrator with a great deal of authority. Knowing how to get things done quickly, he never loses sight of the goal and will make use of everything at hand. While not likely to plunge into new ventures without long, slow thought, he is reliable when pledged. Capricorn natives have a sardonic sense of humor, love good things in life, are responsive to genuine affection. They need approval to show their patient and persistent climb over all obstacles. Their worst characteristic is that they may take advantage of other people while climbing. Starmates: Stalin, Woodrow Wilson, Barry Goldwater, Carl Sandburg, Elvis Presley, Richard Nixon, Martin Luther King, J. Edgar Hoover, Joan of Arc, Nasser, Ari Onassis, Howard Hughes, Humphrey Bogart, and Janis Joplin.

AQUARIUS (January 22-February 18). Here is the philosopher and humanitarian who is gregarious and loyal. Idealistic and progressive, his ideas advance humanity. He may be self-righteous. If thwarted, can be jealous. He is unconventional and creative. He wants to solve the world's problems, but may be too theoretical to act. Starmates: Andrew Jackson, Douglas MacArthur,

Mozart, Franklin Roosevelt, Charles Lindbergh, Abraham Lincoln, Galileo, Edison, Mia Farrow, and Vanessa Redgrave.

PISCES (February 19-March 20). Intensely emotional, passionate, and idealistic, he is resourceful and creative. This is the sign of psychics. He may be so unselfish that people take advantage of him. Also, he is changeable, moody, self pitying, too introverted, and impressionable to his environment. His best trait is sympathy; his worst is an inability to face reality. Starmates: George Washington, Sidney Poitier, Handel, George Harrison, John Steinbeck, Michelangelo, Edward Albee, Einstein, Edgar Cayce, Eileen Garrett, and Elizabeth Taylor.

These capsules supposedly describe every human on earth. Of course, they cannot. They merely take into account the *sun sign* or birthday, but the nature of the signs, the houses, planets, and symbols all have meanings. Popular astrology pours all into a single vessel of terse phrases and generalizations to produce our archetypal Gemini. It would be pure nonsense, except it is accurate enough to create interest.

And interest is swelling. What was once the haunt of tea-cup maidens and overanxious spinsters has become a basic part of the "now" vocabulary. A glance at a pop magazine *Aquarian Astrology for All the Signs* reveals this through titles alone: "Is Early Marriage in Your Stars?" "The Drugless Turn-on," "Your Astrological Potential in College," and "Be a Winner in the Love Game." Another carries a Hollywood gossipfest.

Astrology is now packaging and show biz and exploitation, but, beneath the 12 sign cocktail napkins, it reveals a need for answers. Packaging is important. Sybil Leek's jet setting is more well planned than her books. Glamor must gleam, and seer Maurice Woodruff wafted over the tube for a season.

But astrology has also become a tool in education, especially in Free Universities. The swell of interest is not new. It has occurred in every age that felt confused, uncertain, and in a religious breakdown. Astrologers cleaned up in declining Rome and during seventeenth century plagues. And the young feel as disintegrated and disenchanted as in any previous age. Astrology offers order.

It also produces orders. Carroll Righter, the self styled dean of American astrology appears in 306 newspapers. He has a six figure ascendant. And he is but one of the 10,000 full time astrologers in the United States, not counting computers. Many who are serious astrologers also write astro-potboilers to fill the coffers. Righter's competition includes Sydney Omarr, young with 225 columns. Old and rich is Zolar who doesn't condescend to newspaper slop, but writes much and charges $200 per horoscope.

While supposedly helpful, pop astrology in intent remains largely predictive, whereas serious astrology tries primarily to analyze character and show karmic strengths and shortcomings.

What Is Serious Astrology?

Perhaps the intent of astrology is best summarized by Alan Leo, the theosophist: Houses represent limitations in space; signs, limitations in time; planets, causality or karma. "Those who rule are those who no longer are subject to the great illusions of time, space and causality." Leo assumes a religious view, and astrology began as religion. Whether it was Chaldea or India or Mexico, all with 3000-year-old zodiacs, astrology was religious and it was magic.

Like most of the occult, astrology is based on the greatest analogy—"As above, so below." In ancient times, the spirits or gods of the planets caused actions on earth, fated men's lives.

Without spirits or gods, serious astrology still assumes that the universe is one and man its nucleus. He is affected by everything, especially by the things above, particularly by heavenly bodies closest to him. Astrology was also magic and still can be if people use the influence of the stars for self-interest. Waiting to buy a new car when Uranus and Venus take a certain stance is as magical as poking pins in wax dolls.

Yet, in the glimmering rituals of the past, we have the origin of astrology. It was the ancients who picked the constellations that seemed to affect man most. Why 12 were chosen is forever obscured in antiquity. Yet it was these ancients who created astrology.

As ages passed and Christianity took over, it was thought that fatalism was the worst aspect of astrology. Christians like Origen and St. Augustine railed against fatalistic astrology, and astrologers muttered, "The stars incline, they do not compel." Yet astrology has never escaped the tinge of fatalism because it does predict.

Until the seventeenth century non-fatalistic astrology was not condemned. It was the bailiwick of pope and king, and everyone had an astrologer. Its respectability, its chairs at universities were dealt sneaking blows in this period. Copernicus' heliocentric view made earth-centered astrology seem absurd. *Seem* is important. It did not bother Copernicus or his follower, Tycho Brahe, who predicted the rise and fall of Gustavus Adolphus. It delighted scoffers. Yet a modern scientist, skeptical of astrology, has said to me, "Copernican theory is merely a convenient formula. We may well be whirling round something else." Dane Rudhyar says if we lived on the sun, we would use heliocentric astrology, but we are earth oriented. My scientist and Mr. Rudhyar were not alive, and the Enlightenment drove astrology into the shadow world of gypsy fortune telling.

It was only late in the 19th century that astrology became of interest again. It was explained religiously by the theosophist that as we pass through the spheres, we accumulate rays from each planet. Of course, it was explained scientifically as "vibrations" ruling the universe. While scientific evidence exists for the effects of the moon and sun spots on earth, it is not in science that astrology finds its vindication. Rather, it is in the realm of psychology as proclaimed by Carl Jung and his theory of synchronicity that says all things occurring in space at a certain time take on the quality of that time and of that place. This idea is as old as the unified view of the universe, as new as psychoanalysis. And it is when astrology remains within the realm of explaining our inclinations, our character, that it proves valuable. It is psychic and occult and not empirical. It must be accepted or rejected. But astrology has passed the years from magic to ritual to ridicule to science to religion to psychology.

Delving the Zodiac

Now assume that Mr. Gemini is not satisfied with slop and pop. He begins to buy serious books on the subject. He learns that around the earth each year pass the twelve sun signs of the zodiac in about 30 days per sign, and whirling at different rates around the earth, from the quickness of Mercury to lifeless Pluto, are the planets. On our hub each day, too, the signs pass to create the houses. These are the rudimentary considerations, but all Mr. Gemini can absorb, for he finds himself lost for a time in a quagmire of new words, symbols, and ideas.

The Wheel of Return

Although the vocabulary at first seems strange, Mr. Gemini realizes he is not just sorting out elements, glyphs, symbols, and signs, but that he is participating in a cosmic drama, a wheel that unravels and returns each year. (See chart on pages 32-33.)

The drama begins with **Aries,** a cardinal fire sign. Cardinal signs are all that begin an activity. Fire signs represent energy and spirit. Aries is the irresistible energy of Resurrection and creation. This energy, like the ram who symbolizes the sign, instinctively and intuitively dashes head out, horns down into danger. He is the beginning spirit of creation, the resurrection of spring, as his glyph indicates—a plant shooting forth life, a fountain gushing into spring.

The energy of Aries butts against the stubborn and hostile bull, symbol of **Taurus** where the pure unformed matter of this earth sign remains solid and permanent as all fixed signs solidify and make permanent. Yet the bull is not entirely hostile. It can be yoked to a plow, and Aries' spirit is received as the glyph shows—the circle of unlimited potential surmounted by the horizontal crescent to show receptivity.

Spirit (fire) and matter (earth) meet intelligence (air) in **Gemini** who gyrates to avoid the impossible clash. Because he is an airy intelligent sign, he intuitively but restlessly adjusts to the environment, as should any mutable sign whose function is to search for the new and disintegrate the old. His glyph shows that the intelligence works through discrimination and choice between the two poles of good and evil, spirit and matter. This necessary choice is made clearer by his symbol, the twins, Castor and Pollux, the pure and polluted.

Leaving the intuitive, the cardinal sign of **Cancer** brings the personalizing element of emotion (water) to the intuitive concepts of spirit and matter. It initiates the cycle of the individual who finds life in the world's womb as the glyph's passive dual horizontal lines indicate with their seeds of the new emotional

potential. Similarly, the Crab shows the tenacious grip of emotion on man.

From the watery womb of Cancer emerges the perfect incarnation of man, Adam, in **Leo,** the fixed fire sign, where the golden glow of the fierce fire is now solidified in matter in all its glory. His glyph, the coiled serpent, shows the wisdom and creativity that has produced the first perfect individual. His animal, the lion, shows his mastery. The king of the beasts is like perfect man, strong and conquering. Still in the quarter of emotion, the lion also shows the power of passion and emotion on the individual. Perfect man needs the potential of specific matter as a field of experience.

In **Virgo,** the mutable earth sign, he finds matter organized and transformed into specific things. Virgo's glyph, the Hebrew letter Mem with the added hook, symbol of the fish, reveals that matter has produced. The picture of the virgin who usually carries a sheaf of wheat echoes the miracle of fishes and loaves. And what greater miracle than the fruits of harvest.

Libra, the cardinal air sign initiates the intelligence. Ideal relationship begins as all is harmonious in the scales of Libra whose glyph shows the drawing in of life at sunset where mind and soul are nurtured and prepared. The scales also show man weighing his subjective self against the objective selfless world.

The climax of perfect relationship is the fixed water sign of **Scorpio** where emotional (water) power (fixed) can be constructive regenerators or killers. The glyph shows this function, for to the exalted feminine M is added the barb of cupid's arrow, the last reminder, together with the symbol of the scorpion, of the destructive potential of emotion.

If Scorpio destroys, it merely regenerates and makes way for a new creation, the excitement of Advent, which occurs in the next sign, **Sagittarius.** This is spirit (fire) perfected and diffused (mutable) in many directions for the illumination of all. The glyph shows that the barb has become an arrow, an arrow of aspiration and inspiration propelled by Sagittarius' symbol, the centaur—half man, half beast—who intuitively directs through understanding and takes true aim at the universal.

The universal initiated by **Capricorn.** This cardinal earth sign is perfected matter seeking to materialize all the things of earth and provide for universal good. Its glyph of the serpent encompassing the world shows the universality of matter's perfected wisdom. Its symbol of the mountain goat with the dolphin's tail shows that life must be perfected in matter through experience on all levels.

The perfection of intelligence comes in **Aquarius,** fixed air sign, who desires harmony for all things and shows man solidified, unified by a common ideal. Its glyph, two serpents, waves or electricity show knowledge and intuition harmonized in absolute truth. Similarly, its symbol, the water bearer, carries truth and distills wisdom from knowledge to pour out for all.

And finally the mutable water sign, **Pisces,** shows water and emotion as the universal solvent which dissolves all boundaries and creates chaos. Its glyph of subjective and objective poles inextricably tied but opposed shows there is no possibility of escape from the chaos of Pisces and the symbol of two opposing fish echo this limbo. Fortunately, Pisces, through universal emotion martyrs itself, and water, the source of germination, shoots forth the seeds of Aries and spring and the wheel turns and returns.

The Wanderers

According to astrologers the planets and luminaries of the solar system have definite effects on Mr. Gemini. Generally, the planet which rules his sign is important; more specifically as his horoscope is completed, each planet has meaning and affects his life.

The **Sun** is associated with Apollo. It is the source and sustenance of life—energy incarnate. Alan Leo says it represents the permanent things of life and this may well explain the emphasis on sun signs in pop astrology. The functions of the Sun are vitality, leadership, creativity, the conscious aim and essential inner nature of man. Illumination, stability, and integration could lead to benevolence and nobility or egoism and prodigality. Whatever it causes, it remains the source of life.

The **Moon** rules the night. The goddess Diana and the mysterious are associated with it. Next to the sun, it has the greatest affect on our lives—according to the astrologers. It is associated with tides, menstrual cycles, and even crime rates during the full moon. While the sun integrates, the moon distills, delivering to us the effects of all other planets. Because it is the reflected sun's light, many associate it with the subconscious, instinct, and habit. The moon is the planet of personality, fleeting feelings and imagination, receptivity and impressionability. It leads to sensitivity, adaptability, a sympathetic nature, or to a passive, moody, cautious, and negative personality.

Mercury, the planet closest to the sun, is associated with the messenger of the gods and is erratic as its namesake. Mercury's speed is also associated with quick thoughts and ceaseless activity. Thus, Mercury becomes the transmitter of communication, interpretation, self expression, intelligence, and reason. It enlivens and adds mobility. It can give a quick wit, ingenuity, humor, and a love of research; or it can lead to an irascible temperament—quibbling, picky, superficial, and indecisive.

Venus, the goddess of beauty, is the heavenly sign of man's ability to achieve harmony through intelligence, the arts and social graces. Its activity is to harmonize, beautify, soften and allay man's worries. It causes an affectionate, sympathetic nature, pliant personality or it may seek flattery, luxury and worldly goods. Venus can produce a Mary or a Jezebel.

One must condemn the passion and aggression of **Mars** even though it does cause courage and energy. It also inflames and causes aggression. Little need be said about this warlike planet.

Jupiter is the chief god in mythology; in occultism, it is often called the Christ within. It shows the higher mind, wisdom, expansiveness, optimism, spontaneity, and a willingness to gather experience. Its activity is to expand, multiply, preserve, and cause increase on all levels of existence.

Saturn tests people and thus, through sound and dislike of its karmic tests, people ally Saturn and Satan. Saturn's rings symbolize the limitations imposed by the planet's actions that mean harsh discipline for many. It is, perhaps, the most karmic of the planets and at best gives responsibility, justice, and stability; at worst, ambition, self-preservation, pessimism, and caution.

The Higher Octaves

The three outer planets—Uranus, Neptune, and Pluto—are recent discoveries in 4000 year terms. Their relationship and influence on man is unclear or slight. Generally, **Uranus** acts to break up the solidity of Saturn. It thus represents originality, inspiration, independence, inventiveness, and the ability to synthesize.

Neptune, associated with the sea god means space and water—intuition, hypersensitivity, imagination. It transcends boundaries into limitless expansion, idealism, sympathy and compassion. It is the planet of the martyr and the psychic.

Pluto, god of the underworld and last discovered of the planets, shows man's underworld consciousness, unredeemed and unintegrated.

The Houses

The year unravels the zodiac. The signs are related to time. You are an Aries, a Libra, a Scorpio whether born in Bengal or Boston. The day also spins through the zodiac. Before Mr. Gemini can make the final step in erecting his horoscope, he must know where he fits into his place on earth. It is simple enough to know where you are born, but with the whirl of all signs every 24 hours, you must also know the exact time of your birth.

While it would be natural to begin house 1 with the sign of Aries, the passage of time seldom permits. Rather time of birth might put Sagittarius in House 1 and the other 11 houses would be assigned and numbered anti-clockwise according to the signs following Sagittarius. House One is called the Ascendant and next to the moon and sun sign is the most important part of the horoscope. It indicates bodily form, physical appearance and the means by which the native expresses himself most naturally. The ascendant is the beginning of life, the awareness of self and the subjective. It is the seed of our being from which we grow. The other traditional meanings of the houses are shown in the chart on the opposite page.

The complexity of house meanings cannot be shown in such a brief space. Neither can the other important but complex details be described. Aspects, detriments, intercepted signs all become familiar terms to the astrologer. But combining the traditional and this cursory philosophic may help you to understand the man traveling around the wheel from self to not-self,

Table of Houses

subjective to objective, intuition to reason. Like the zodiac it is a never ending wheel and cycle of return, a karmic pattern which man must comprehend and overcome. Now, Mr. Gemini may construct his horoscope and find not just himself, but—according to astrology—an orderly and cosmic pattern for his life.

3 THE SILVER KEY:

THE TAROT

Have you ever heard playing cards called the devil's pasteboards? That's because they are associated with fortune telling. Our present day playing cards are really an outgrowth of an earlier deck called the Tarot. Their intent was not devilish but divine: to teach wisdom. These 78 cards with their wealth of concrete symbolism were long obscured in elite salons, but now are common possessions of housewives who liven up a coffee klatsch with "fortunes." Their appeal to youth is even greater. A rock group is named The Fool for one of the cards. A rock musical, *Tarot,* opened in December, 1970. Like many aspects of the occult, the Tarot has been perverted in purpose throughout the ages.

Originally, the cards, speaking a symbolic language, were for initiation. If the stars of astrology indicated inclinations at birth, the Tarot showed how to overcome shortcomings and enter into enlightenment. The initiation might take a lifetime or be accomplished quickly by a great mind who comprehends the wisdom and necessity of each card.

The source of this wisdom and means for initiation is shrouded in myth. Some claim the fantastic age of 35,000 years and their origination on the legendary continents of Atlantis and Mu, whose refugees after the continents sank to watery beds delivered them to China, India, and Egypt. Egypt, especially, seems the home of the Tarot, and it is claimed that the ancient book, *The Emerald Tablets of Hermes Trismegistus,* was a discourse on the symbols of the cards. Others attribute Hebraic origins and link them to Jewish mysticism. Whatever the origin of the Tarot, a universal language of symbols was being worked out. It was a language studied since earliest time, entering history in 1392. It became the subject of serious modern study influencing men like T. S. Eliot and C. J. Jung.

Although the cards may be used for divination, our first interest is in their initiatory purpose. Here we need discuss only 22 of the cards, the Major Arcana. The remainder are primarily divinatory and will be discussed later. The 22 Arcana of Initiation basically represent the dualistic forces man must overcome and reconcile. Their symbolic path shows an arduous climb to the heights of initiation.

The Path of the Material

The paths of initiation are divided into three sections. Each ascends higher into the initiatory ranks. The first seven steps and cards lead one out of the illusion of the material. God becomes human in the perfect man (Arcanum I. *The Magus)* who through will and intelligence plunges towards the hidden wisdom of the feminine (II. *Veiled Isis).* But the hidden wisdom is that life has a dual nature. The perfect man and perfect woman uniting will and wisdom produce the activity and creativity of life (III. *Isis Unveiled),* which they rule. Their rule is through the realization of earthly sovereignty (IV. *The Sovereign)* or in Spiritual Inspiration (V. *The Hierophant).* Either means of rulership leads inevitably to a choice (VI. *The Two Paths)* and man chooses the earth and fails or chooses the spirit and is victorious over matter (VII. *The Conqueror)* and ready to travel higher on the path of initiation.

From a single glance you can see that the arcana rest heavily on a system of astrological, numerical, symbolic, hiero-

glyphic, and color correspondences. A presentation of the first seven arcana in greater detail shows the path more clearly. Let us look first at I. **The Magus.** The number 1 and the letter A symbolize God in manifestation. The planet Mercury means intelligence. The Magus' white robe shows his purity. The serpent entwined round his waist is the symbol of eternal wisdom. Putting these correspondences together gives us a clearer picture of Arcanum I: Perfect man, untempted Adam, robed in white, crowned with a golden band as the spiritual organs awake in his head. Before him is a cage containing an Ibis, symbol of the god of intelligence and magic. On the table are four necessary elements for creation. The first initiatory step is to possess intelligence, power, and will to create purely: he points with his scepter upwards to the source of his divine intelligence and the place to which he aspires. His left hand points downward, to the material he must overcome.

To conquer matter, one must understand, and the Magus meets the feminine principle, II. **The Veiled Isis.** Associated with Virgo, she is the perfect feminine, unfallen Eve, but she is also the protectress of a secret, the secret of ever-playing duality as she sits between the columns of the positive and the negative. The hidden wisdom is symbolized by the veil over her face, but also by the book, half hidden in her lap. Her wisdom must be sought, and she must be prepared; the crescent on her head shows the necessary receptivity of the female. So the second step is mental, the knowledge of the ever-changing polarities of life, but also we see the perfect female receptive to the perfect male.

With the marriage of the Magus and Isis Veiled we find the exalted feminine in III. **Isis Unveiled.** She has succeeded in divine creation. Seated on a cubic stone, the symbol of matter she has overcome, Isis is surrounded by the light of the sun and

its creativity. Her crown is the 12 stars of the zodiac; her feet rest on the moon, the matter she has created and conquered.

But how can even submissive or divine matter be ruled? Arcanum IV, **The Sovereign,** gives one answer: the *duty* to realize earthly potentials and rule them. How he shall rule is indicated by the scepter surmounted by the circle of spirit and the wisdom he attained from above. It is indicated by the left hand pointing to the substance he must rule and eventually overcome. The serpent now crowns his head as eternal wisdom rises higher. Materialism has been mastered on an earthly plane.

Now, it must be achieved spiritually, the function of **The Hierophant,** Arcanum V. Spiritual wisdom is tested in liberty of action. Seated beneath the canopy, he understands the mysteries of duality and the elements—the columns and two figures at his feet. The design of his staff shows the mastery of three worlds—physical, mental, spiritual—as he pierces the earth with it. His right hand is raised in the esoteric blessing. The entire arcanum shows mastery and triumph.

But mastery could be used for good or evil. The choice must be made between material and the higher world as indicated in VI. **The Two Paths.** Standing motionless at the crossroads, hands folded on chest, eyes on ground, a youth must choose between the maiden on the right (spirit) and the one on the left (sensuality). The consequence the youth cannot see is death with the arrow of the sun directed at the vice. The complete balance and lack of motion also indicates that man must not only choose, but also harmonize the two forces in his life.

If the right choice is made, victory is assured over the material, and the victor rides the chariot of Osiris in VII. **The Conqueror.** He has triumphed with the sword and scepter now raised in victory. The four columns indicate his victory over the four elements, and the conquest of dualism is shown by the harnessed sphinxes of good and evil who carry him forward. One path of initiation is passed, another just to begin.

The Path of Self

It would be easy to bask in the perfected self. But pride and thus downfall would result. So, as the chariot indicates, the initiate must travel onward to sacrifice his ego.

The self is in perfect harmony as Arcanum VIII. *The Balance* shows. She weighs all things—good against evil, self against selflessness. To overcome the self, however, one needs the detachment, wisdom and self-sufficiency of IX. *The Sage* or *Hermit.* One must accept the karmic pattern, the eternal flux of X. *The Wheel of Fortune.* Detachment and acceptance give him the power and discipline (XI. *The Enchantress)* to voluntarily submit the ego to martyrdom (XII. *The Hanged Man)* and accept death (XIII. *The Reaper),* which is really a transformation (XIV. *The Alchemist)* from ego to selflessness, raising the initiate beyond the tomb to infinite bliss.

The Balance, Arcanum VIII, begins the process of change as shown by the scales in her left hand. They are in perfect balance, not yet tipped by man's good or evil deeds. That the weighing is impartial is shown by her bandaged eyes. The lifted sword is equally impartial as a protection for the good, a warning for the evil. At this stage, the initiate prefers no course of action, but action is inevitable.

Since man cannot rest in the Balance with his conception of the true self, he moves and becomes IX. **The Sage** or **Hermit.** Now an elderly philosopher carries a partially concealed lantern; wisdom is never won easily. His staff shows that he is a wanderer through the world of conquered matter. His cloak shows that it is wise to keep this wisdom to himself as illusion is still possi-

ble. This may lead to isolation, but also to detachment from the self. This detachment is necessary for acceptance of karma and the unexplainable patterns of life.

Arcanum X. **The Wheel of Fortune** is karma in action. The impassive sphinx has the arrow ready to strike right or left— Hermanulus, the spirit of good striving toward the top of the wheel who may be prideful or the Typhon, spirit of evil, being cast down as the wheel turns.

Once the abyss of karma is accepted, one must submit to the disciplines of moral force as in XI. **The Enchantress.** A young maiden (wisdom) unites with the lion (love). She closes his jaws without effort, a symbol of discipline and moral strength. With detachment from self, acceptance of karma, and subjection to divine will, one is ready for the final step of selflessness—sacrifice.

Arcanum XII. **The Hanged Man** shows the self sacrifice for a higher goal. The man hangs by one foot from the gallow which rests between the two trunks of good and evil. His legs form a cross, symbol of the material world to which he has been sacrificed, and coins, his earthly goods, drop to the ground.

Selflessness accepted and complete, the Initiate waits only for XIII. **The Reaper.** This grim skeleton with his swinging scythe shows the fleetingness of life. The grisly hands and feet are reminders of man reaping as he sowed. But, behind the reaper shines a rainbow, the promise of renewal and transformation. And the heads and the feet grow up as fast as they are cut down. This transformation to a higher plane is the initiate becoming the celestial man.

This new being is shown in Arcanum XIV. **The Alchemist,** where a handsome youth stands in the sun pouring ceaselessly the liquids of a golden urn (male) to a silver one (female). Male and female have become meaningless as they are endlessly mixed

and transmuted to the higher plane of celestial beings as shown by the airy wings on the Alchemist. Another path.

The Path from Fatality

Perhaps, the hardest illusion to overcome is that all things are fated. Even celestial man might balk if he believed that time, decay, death ruled all. Arcanum XV. *The Typhon* is a foul reminder of such fatality. It may also seem that all deeds are doomed to outward failure as XVI. *The Lightning Struck Tower* would indicate. But, beyond the ruin is either hope for the man who can overcome fatality in the tranquility of XVII, *The Star* or disappointment in the twilight of XVIII. *The Moon.* Accepting duality in fate as in the other paths is necessary to find the happiness of XIX. *The Sun,* where man no longer fears judgment (XX. *The Sarcophagus)* since it is merely another transformation. From the tomb arises XXI. *The Adept,* eternally renewed and totally initiated.

Fatality is well symbolized by XV. **The Typhon,** more hideous than any Christian "devil." With the body of a hippopotamus, the head of a crocodile, the wings of a bat, and the feet of a goat, he brandishes his torch over the two chained men at his feet. He has broken the two columns; there is neither good nor evil, only chaos and the tyrannic rule of his iron scepter. If one cannot accept something beyond fate, perhaps faith, he is chained to the Typhon.

Or he may feel the doom of XVI. **The Lightning Struck Tower.** It may signify the Tower of Babel, built by man's pride only to be ruined by a higher power, one which respects no station as a crowned and uncrowned man fall from the tower to pay karmic debts.

15   XV   ♄

ו   X   ♑

16   XVI   ♂

ה   O   ♍

17   XVII   ♒

פ   F-P-PH   ♓

18   XVIII   ☉

צ   SH-TS-TZ   ♏

51

Before all is lost, an arcanum of hope appears, XVII. **The Star.** The figure kneels with one foot on water, the other on land, equally at home in either element, and pours the fruits of the Alchemist's mixture on land and sea. Behind the figure grows a plant with three lotus blossoms representing perfection. Resting on the flower is a butterfly, symbol of eternity. Shining over all is the eight-rayed star. The divided triangle shows that just as there is light above, so will it shine below if one continues in perfection, expectation, and hope.

If one abandons hope, he must face the disappointment of XVIII. **The Moon.** Here two white and black, good and evil, pyramids stand. The white one has a door, for only good may be fathomed. The sole light is the vaguely hidden moon at which the dogs bay hopelessly. The crab is equally futile; he cannot crawl from his place and can merely sting.

Yet overcoming disappointment at the hands of karmic life leads to earthly happiness in XIX. **The Sun.** Here celestial man and woman are united in the glory of the bright sun. They stand protected by a circle of flowers and are perfectly innocent, fearing neither life nor death. Ready to accept all, including the call to judgment (XX. **The Sarcophagus),** their final renewal. Here the angel in the sun sounds his trumpet, and from the coffin spring three figures, child, woman, and man, all the stages of life consummated. The newly expanded consciousness becomes the helper of all, XXI. **The Adept,** who has received the eternal reward of playing the strings on the harp of body, mind, and spirit, protected by the four strong signs of the zodiac and a circle of lotus blossoms. All duality is erased, fatality left behind in the reward of the adept. But, except for the extraordinary, it is clear the path is steep, the rewards tenuous, and the choices narrow.

The Floater

Arcanum XXII. **The Materialist** or **The Fool,** is the floater of the arcana. The Materialist walks toward the crocodile, blind and unaware of light or dark. He could precede the Magus and be the unawakened man called to initiation. Or, he could be dropped any place in the path when the wrong choice is made. Given a new interpretation, he might seal the deck as the divine clown who is beyond caring about the dangers of crocodiles, duality, or wisdom. This ancestor of the joker may be no fool at all unless he is a holy fool.

The Tarot for Divination

While some find the Tarot most meaningful as a path of initiation and a means of meditation, its primary modern usage is fortune telling. Based on the analogy of "as below, so above," the Tarot is used to determine the divine will at a particular moment. Tarot readings may be surprisingly accurate. When they are, I suspect it is the psychic mind at work using the cards for concentration as they form an intuitive pattern. However the Tarot works, its usage for divination is an important modern manifestation of the occult.

But to discuss the cards for divination, we must consider the remaining 56 cards of the deck. In addition to the 22 major arcana are the 56 minor arcana, basically modifications and interpretations of the Major 22. These 56 cards are arranged in four suits: Wands (clubs), signifying enterprise and glory; Cups (hearts), emotions; Swords (spades), strife and misfortune; and Pentacles (Diamonds), truth and money. Twelve of the minor arcana are called court cards being Kings, Queen, Knights, and Pages. They may represent the physical appearance of the questioner, his or her marital status, or, more significantly, his zodiacal sign. For example, the Kings of Wands is a man of Aries temperament. The meaning of the minor arcanum relies on the major arcana to which it is attached. For example, the six of cups (emotions) relates to Arcanum VI. *The Two Paths* and indicates a love affair. Further, a minor arcanum following a major one in a reading where the numbers do not correspond, modifies the meaning of the lesser. Let us assume that XII, the Hanged Man, immediately precedes the six of cups. This would indicate that the love affair would be sacrificed and possibly one would feel martyred.

It should also be mentioned that there are not just many cards, but many decks. Too many reflect Medieval Christianity rather than the more ancient symbolism. For this reason, I have discussed the Egyptian deck with its older synthesis of symbols, letters, and analogies.

Preparing to Read

A Tarot reading may be mysterious and mystic. Your reader may mumble about "vibrations," tell you not to touch the cards except when told since his vibrations are in them. He may pull his cards from a box wrapped in silk appropriate to his zodiacal sign. Such reverence for the cards reveals them not as tools for concentration but as objects worthy in themselves of awe and reverance. I still consider it liberation day when my wife, in a fit of disgust, tore up a deck of Tarot and stamped on them. The vibrations killed neither of us.

Assume that a Tarot reading is to occur. You may ask a question of the reader. He will select a spread, an arrangement of cards in a pattern, suitable to your question from the simplicity of a five card horizontal spread for a simple yes-no question to a complicated life spread of 50. The spreads are usually laid right to left and turned over as each card is interpreted. Since the cards are based on an elaborate system of correspondences, you may wait as the reader ponders the many analogies. For example, the nine of wands connects to the Major Arcanum of the Sage. This brings illumination, particularly since the card is associated with the sun. The card is also associated with Sagittarius and Aquarius who aspire toward universal service and friendship. This would indicate that the hermit is seeking friendship. The association with Jupiter and Leo might indicate a profitable friendship. So, to gather all these associations, it may be a long time before your reader says, "You will receive illumination through a wise and profitable friendship." Even this is oversimplified and, of course, modified by the remainder of the spread.

The Tarot and You

Like astrology, then, the Tarot is used for initiation, as a path to wisdom, and for divination, as a way of predicting the future. In either case this offer of wisdom and insight into the future has great appeal in a time of rapid change and uncertainty, when traditional religious values are being challenged. Both astrology and the Tarot come cloaked in the myths and symbols of ancient ages and seem to offer the security of a long link with the past. In a technological age and a superorganized church they meet for many the need for mystery and hope and order.

4 THE COMBINATION LOCK:

NUMEROLOGY

As prospective parents pour over the lists of Abigails and Jennifers, Reubens and Jasons, they don't realize how close to the occult they are. Yet this careful choosing of names is a magical link that ties them to the most primitive man, for the importance of the name is the secret of numerology.

Numerology roots in many occult beliefs. The belief that a name contains one's inner essence is only one. This link could serve for destruction and, as late as the 15th century, sorcerers believed that writing a person's name on a piece of paper and burying it, would kill the person. Nor is the Bible free from this fear of the magical link. Recall the angel who wrestled Jacob or the one who visited Samson's father. Neither would give his name. Indeed, the Bible alone shows how significant numbers are in Western culture. Consider the careful measurements for the Temple. Think of the close attention to the years of each patriarch. The Bible contains an entire book called "Numbers." And think of all the three's and seven's and twelve's and one thousand's. On another plane, how many still fear the number 13? And maybe in a world where we are spindled, stapled, and mutilated by numbers, it is comforting to think they have some meaning.

The modern numerologist no longer buries names to destroy men. Rather, he likes to reveal and be scientific. Although numerology is more an art of analogy—the name is like the person, being a miniature of him—Senor Numero would rather talk about vibrations and tell you that everything vibrates at a different rate of speed, so your essential nature is determined by your rate of vibration.

The historical root of this analogy is not with electricity, but with the Greek philosopher, Pythagoras (c. 530 B.C.) who believed in reincarnation and magic, but who also discovered that musical intervals are based on time. This suggested to him that the way from chaos to order was mathematical and all confusion could be reduced to numbers. The numbers 1-9 he sanctified as whole numbers; after them mere repetition begins. Pythagoras and the centuries which follow accept another occult belief—dualism. Odd numbers are male and good; even, female, dull, and usually bad. (Apologies to women's lib).

So, we have a universe connected in a great mathematical pattern: the belief that a name of a thing contains its essence. According to the numerologist we just need a method to reduce the name to numbers and we have the answers of the universe, or at least a key to our character.

It is in the reduction of names to numbers that disagreement first arises. Modern numerological systems list the numbers 1-9 and the alphabet in order beneath. But the alphabet and numbers have so long been separate in our language that many dislike the idea. Turning to the Hebrew alphabet where there were no numbers, but where each letter had its numerical equivalent, is more comforting. Since Hebrew lacks an e, i, j, o, x, numerologists turn to the Greek alphabet sanctified by Pythagoras and use their numerical equivalents. The system is as follows:

1	2	3	4	5	6	7	8
A	B	C	D	E	U	O	F
I	K	G	M	H	V	Z	P
Q	R	L	T	N	W		
J		S			X		
Y							

Since less than half the letters equal the same in both systems, numerologists give different interpretations to the same name. Maybe the sanctity of age gives more credence to the Hebrew system, which I use for all examples in this chapter:

$$\begin{matrix} J & a & n & e & t & & R & i & n & g & d & a & h & l \\ 1 & +1 & +5 & +5 & +4 & + & 2 & +1 & +5 & +3 & +4 & +1 & +5 & +3 & =40 \end{matrix}$$

The total has more than two figures. Since this is repetitious, it must be reduced to its digital root. To do this you merely add $4+0=4$ and find that Janet is a Number Four person. If your name contains the essence of you, your birthday shows the vibrations of the universe branded on you at birth. Janet was born on January 3, 1940. She is $1+3+1+9+4+0=18=1+8=9$. A nine birth. Two other important numbers concern the numerologist. The value of the vowels is your heart number, the hidden you, springing from the analogy that the Hebrews had no vowels and they were thus "hidden." The value of the consonant adds your outer personality. How do we ever consolidate Janet's numbers? I leave it to Pythagoras.

The Purpose of Numbers

The primary purpose of numerology is character analysis: to discover what the above has to say to us below. But it is also a means for self-improvement. Once the numbers are known and your name is a six, you should do all important things on days that add to six (6, 15, 24). Or you might bet on a horse carrying the number 6. Even diet may be based on numbers. An apple, for example, should be good for a number seven person since its digital root is also seven.

Limitless possibilities. Your city should be considered through vowels as expression of its inner nature. London suits a five person, for it has many sidedness and resilience. Even your street address should add to a proper number.

Yet if all goes wrong, you have one recourse. Change your name. Medieval Jews changed names of the dying to trick the angel of death. While most numerologists disclaim such superstition, they also like to point to the importance of name changes. Originally, Napoleon Buonaparte, led as a *one* should with energy and ambition. With the dropping of the "u" to sound more French, he became a *four,* the number of defeat. But you may be more interested in your name than Napoleon's.

The Meaning Is in the Numbers

One. Leadership of the numbers leads to the analogy of leadership of men, origination and invention, as does its association with the Sun. Since one cannot be divided by any other number, the one person is granted the highest fixity of purpose leading to success. One is also the number of Jehovah and a one is as single-minded as Jehovah in creating or demanding complete obedience. Like Jehovah one is the unmoved mover, the bedrock of all action, and shares the qualities of authority, creativity, power, and honor. Two other characteristics spring from less obvious analogies. There is little interest in friendship because the number stands alone. It is creative because one added to any other odd number produces an even—a new and opposite creation—the feminine.

Two. Our first feminine number associated with the Moon, adds the niceties of life: a soft and quiet nature, taking responsibility for others. Since two follows one, the analogy is that they like to serve. But, as the moon has its dark side, so does two, one of the most unlucky numbers possible no matter how much numerologists love praise and gloss over the evil.

It is the entrance of the feminine into our numbers, and like Eve, the second creation, brings evil. While these dark aspects are usually glossed over with "moodiness, dark temper," it is apparent that two has many bad associations. The devil has not five toes, but a cloven hoof. St. Augustine observed that the unclean beasts entered the ark by twos; the cleans by sevens.

Three. It is associated with Jupiter the most fortunate planet and the planet of religion. It is the number of the Trinity and of the Resurrection day. It is connected with the first three commandments—all concerning God. Yet, I also associate three with Venus as it is the planet and number of creation, since three reconciles the opposing forces of one and two, creating harmony and a love of beauty. It might even be associated with Mercury, for the three is described as brilliant and imaginative, versatile and energetic, an able and witty communicator. Three's worst faults are a tendency to overextend efforts and the desire for the approval of others. Because three is such a fortunate number, we find it in magic as the number of completeness. Who needs more than three guesses? In magic, it is particularly effective for love philtres, and to repeat an incantation three times is sufficent.

Four. We flow back to evil and feminine, doubly evil because it is 2 x 2, the double feminine. It is bad analogically because there are four elements, which produce dull and lifeless matter, tying us to this earthly existence. Fours are solid like matter, thus practical people. So tied to earth, they lack creative nature, but are organizers. As one would expect, they are "down to earth," steady and respectable, given to routine, detail, and hard work. Associated with Saturn, they may be stern, grim, even repressive like the tester of the planets. They possess Saturnine melancholy and even have outbursts of rage. So Number Fours, although numerologists like to gloss over it, are doomed to poverty, misery, and defeat.

The number may be bad for the occultist, for here the goal is to transcend matter, but for a Christian, matter is not evil and form is the way from chaos. I think Christianity bears out the worth of the material with the Four Gospels, the four lettered name of God, YHVH, and the holy "four-square" city in Revelation.

Five. I sense this number tizzies numerologists. It must be good, but so much of it sounds bad. The associations with Mercury sound generally good, for it creates the adventurous and attractive, the clever and the lover of travel and new surroundings. That he is restless and impatient, existing on nervous energy, is not really bad, nor is his versatility. But lurking beneath the surface goodness, I see many reminders of the negative, perhaps in association with Mars: Five may be irresponsible, inconsiderate, and self-indulgent. Five is also associated with sex (Mars in Scorpio) because it combines the feminine two and the masculine three. Our five senses may lead to delight, but it is also the number of sexual excess and even perversion. This ambivalence of good and evil may be because the number stands halfway through the digits, balancing good and evil. But even the Bible shows its mixed blessing. Christ, while warned of the Crucifixion five times, was also injured five times after his arrest. Ironically, in modern times our leaders are five star generals, and the temple of Mars is the Pentagon.

Six. If you expect the dark and feminine, you are wrong; six is a good number because it is three doubled, the perfected feminine. Like Venus, it dispenses harmony and peace, happiness and kindliness. Being the doubled three, it is also a balancer and equable. I am almost bored by listing the good points of a six: friendly, loyal, upright, sincere, wholehearted. It is little wonder that with their string of exquisite superlatives, their faults may be smugness and self-satisfaction, obstinacy and conceit.

Good analogies are also clear in the Bible. Man labors six days, then rests. And what greater blessing than man's creation on the sixth day. Pythagoras also sanctifies the number as "the perfection of parts."

Seven. It is the number of the philosopher and mystic, the occultist and the scholar because of its connection with Uranus, Aquarius, and the cycle of the moon. It is the number of completeness as creation was completed in seven days.

But it is also the number of the natural hermit because seven cannot be produced by multiplication and stands aloof from the other numbers. As the seventh day was for rest and meditation, the seven person wishes to withdraw and meditate. Other characteristics naturally follow: dignity, self control, seriousness, great intellect. The faults also follow naturally. The recluse number is bad at expressing himself, and his meditation on the follies of man may lead to pessimism, aloofness, superiority, and sarcasm.

Biblically, consider the seven commandments dealing with the ethics of man. Joshua marched seven times round Jericho. There are seven petitions in the Lord's Prayer, the seven gifts of the holy spirit, and the famous forgiveness of 70 x 7. Seven is the number of completion and seems to summarize all earthly existence with 70 years as the span of life, seven ages of man, seven days, colors, and stages of growth. And so seven may well end our life on earth as governed by its earthly cycles and rhythms.

Eight. This is often considered the number of the spectacular success or failure. It is the troublesome four doubled. But here the energy, associated with Mars, spurs one through the toils. It remains feminine, and the high shooter may end in spectacular failure. This combination leads to worldly involvement, a thirst for power and money, which can create successful businessmen and politicians. Although strong, tough, and practical, it may lead downward to materialism, selfishness, tyranny, and even wild rebelliousness.

Eight is dualistic as the two circles indicate. The other face of worldly involvement is shown by the fact that it represents the life beyond with seven completing the earthly cycle. It is interesting that eight on its side is the mathematical and occult symbol of infinity. Eight also represents new life. Man has seven orifices, woman an eighth — the orifice through which life enters. Religion seems to recognize this fact. Judaism names a baby boy on the eighth day. Christianity baptizes the child in an octagonal font.

Nine. The attributes of nine are largely based on the idea that it is the multiple of the good three. Its high mental and spiritual attitude produces visionary, idealistic, even psychic personalities. Nines make good scientists, teachers, and artists. In its shortcomings, nine may be egotistical since nine multiplied by any number inevitably returns to nine. Example of *nine* personalities are Lincoln and Kennedy. This should prove it is a number of completeness and high mindedness. Finally, it is the number of initiation, for it stands at the end of the series, a series that can only be repeated on a higher scale.

Objections

A source of occult art with no common system or agreement of interpretation is suspect and open to many objections. What about numerical systems themselves? Also, our name is a chance affair. Numerologists say no. There is no chance, for each person is the product of the combining forces of the universe. Before birth, the universe stamps the child's character and destiny so strongly on parents' minds that they choose the right name. An alternative idea is that the soul chooses a body with the proper name.

What do we do with the fact that we have many names? The name on our birth certificate; a first, middle, and last name; the nicknames that please or plague us; a woman's married name. Simple. All names are examined. Your full name at birth especially shows the forces of the universe on you, but each subsequent name marks a stage of development and expresses your character. Further, our eminent numerologist would say that each letter and its number should be examined. If a number is missing or appears too often, as *two* in Hitler, you'd better change your name!

More serious objections are also wiped away in the realm of birth numbers. Each person born on the same day will have the same destiny. Numerologists insert the name here and say destiny is combined with name and year. Most serious is the source of the calendar. Much of the world uses a different one and even our own is of a very recent date (sixth century A.D.) and is agreed to be inaccurate since Christ was probably born in 4 B.C. The reform of the calendar in 1582 further complicates things. But numerologists say it is the year of our Lord and not the year of change that counts.

In spite of the silliness, superstition, even fatalism of the art, numerology is an interesting study. It affects much of the occult, and is a good analogous branch of it. Numerological symbols are significant in literature, including the literature of the Bible.

5 SOME SKELETON KEYS:

SLACK MAGIC

As below, so above, gives rise to some of the most ridiculous antics of the occult. Since man is the image of what is above, all parts of him must be important. From the grab bag of occult tricks comes one to show absurdity amuck: moleosophy claims that through the location, shape, and color of a mole, a person's character may be judged and his future indicated. In shape, round moles are good; angular, bad. In color, light are good; black, "Difficult." By location, a mole on the ankle indicates a man of fearful nature; on the arms, courteous, happy; on the ear, riches far beyond expectation. Ridiculous, but as late as 1946 lengthy treatises were written on the significance of moles. C. Tousey Taylor, who claimed the Devil's death in 1846, also gloriously contributes a means for finding the tribe of Israel to which we belong from the location of our most prominent mole. Find it, then note the part of the body, find its rulership in the zodiac and abracadabra find your tribe. I must confess that I peeked: I belong to the tribe of Gad. If you, too, are a peeker, you will find that a shoulder mole is the tribe of Dan; a head mole, Asher; a chest mole, Issacher; a stomach mole, Judah; a left thigh, Simeon, a right, Reuben; a right calf, Benjamin; a left, Joseph; back and hip, Zebulon and Levi; and a foot, Naphtali. If you have no moles, perhaps you are Norwegian.

Bumpology

In the latter part of the eighteenth century, Dr. Franz Gall invented phrenology. In 1796, he presented his theories based on extensive research. Gall classified 26 bumps, his followers more. And phrenology peaked with the Brothers Fowler, who, busy with calipers measuring head bumps, traveled across the skulls of America, issued charts and eventually set up a phrenological museum with thousands of human skulls.

Most of phrenology was silly, some barbaric such as calipering poor inmates of asylums to discover disturbed heads, and convicts for the criminal type. Yet I could not resist mentioning this occult "art."

Silver My Greasy Palm

Palmistry, with much tradition behind it and a good deal of theory dating back to China, is a more reputable art than moles and bumps. Theoretically! In practice it is often the shoddiest of occult arts. Based still on the analogy of the human body, it follows the principle of *as above, so below*. Palmistry teaches that the lines on our palms were impressed at birth by cosmic rays and show our character. The reverse analogy is more true, from our hands we can tell our fate.

The art has two categories. Chirognomy studies the shape of the hands, and chiromancy, the lines and mounts of the palm. Chirognomy has various classifications of fingers. A square palmed, short fingered hand is the Practical Hand, heavy, solid, coarse, slow, and primitive. It is close to sub-human. The Intuitive or Psychic hand distinguishes itself with a long palm and short fingers. It, being a step above the practical, relies on intuition, which for the psychic is good. The sensitive hand reveals both long fingers and a long palm. It is the artistic, elegant hand of the artist stretching across the keyboard, flourishing the brush, molding the clay. Dürer's "Praying Hands" is often used as an example. Many would like the intellectual hand with its square palm and long fingers. And watch out for dirty fingernails.

The lines, so fateful, are of interest to most people. These "graffiti of the skies," as a Chinese palmist called them, show just about everything. We've all looked at our life lines to see whether or not we will see three score and ten. The life line should be high and strong and reach down to the thumb's base. Differences in measurement show the length of our life. And I have read in all seriousness that Christ's line ended with a large circle at the measurement of 33. The head line begins above the life line or is connected to it. Again, the longer the line, the better the head. Next is the heart line. Beginning around the first finger it can indicate many loves; if between the second and third, it may mean that the person is cold. If it joins the head line, you guessed it — the heart rules the head. The line of Saturn or fate shows good or bad luck, usually bad, but the line of Apollo adds brilliance and strength to the fate line as a good Sun should. The line of Mercury governs health. If you want to be healthy, you should have a strong line beginning at the base of the wrist and reaching to the little finger. The bracelets or rascettes on the wrist measure life, too — 25 years per rascette. If you have bad grooves, I can suggest nothing but a good engraver.

Seriously, I object to this emphasis on fate, counting, and measuring out our days. But, in addition to the fated theories of palmistry, I object more strongly to much of its practice. It usually occurs in nightclubs or bars where Mr. Phalange comes over after you've tipped a few. He asks a question, you spill out your life story. He repeats it and you may as well have been wearing a glove.

I'm Seeing Red!

Rush right out and buy your aura goggles!!! Only $24.50. This occult art based on the analogy of the body has the theory that each body emanates a certain colored aura, which reveals character and even health. The importance of colors is ancient. We know that primitive man daubed red, the color of blood, to bring bravery before battle. For some reason, the Druids chose blue. We know half the world was traded away for brightly colored trinkets. And we know astrology assigns colors to each sign and planet. More recently, psychological studies have shown that people deprived of green, the color of nature, soon go "stir crazy."

But, it is a far leap to say that each of us vibrating at a different rate produces a different colored aura. A true psychic may well be able to see this aura as Edgar Cayce could, but the method in common practice is shoddy to say the least.

Dowse and Dangle

Rhabdomancy or dowsing is one of the few even semi-respectable occult arts that is based on the magic link: a branch of nature seeks through nature to find its element. Dowsing is one of the means of finding water or metal with a rod. It assumes the operator makes no movement, aims at passivity, and allows himself to be acted upon from without or within. This is rhabdomancy in its harmless form, merely seeking water with a forked stick. The introduction of the pendulum produced radiesthesia in which either the pendulum or the stick may be used to find the element. But harmless. However, the rod and the pendulum have also been used to diagnose diseases, spotting malignant areas in man, and curing them with imitative links. I do not wish to discount psychic healing, since Jesus and the Apostles were practitioners, but willow rod and pendulum cannot replace the x-ray or the iron lung.

Psychic Myopia

Climb the stairs to a dark room and find a frowsy haired, worn out psychic and pretend you are participating in the art of *scrying*. The future's in there. Just look for it. There is nothing in there, and you are in the realm of the psychic, for the crystal ball is only a tool for concentration. The gazer may achieve a trance of sorts combining telepathy, remembrances, precognition, and dreams. Serious psychics have gazed into the ball and found only shadowy images. It is not likely that Madame Sosostris with 16 clients a day can see more. The lights are low, the draperies thick, the atmosphere decayed, the future bright, and the cost high. But you at least are granted free will in scrying. You make the gazings true or false. Although this may be the backdoor of the psychic, it is usually worn out, and only if the ball is used as a source of concentration, is it remotely valid.

Mene, Mene Tekel Upharsin!

Another release of psychic energy is through our handwriting. As early as 1622, Camillo Baldo began to study handwriting. I cannot possibly show or even discuss the loops and swirls, the size and shape that became characteristic of a personality. Each slope, each slant, each loop, dropped *t* and undotted *i* has significance. While the psychic theory may well be that the inner being flows through the hand, psychologists have done much study and find remarkable similarities between character and writing. (My own impossible scrawl ranges from schizophrenic to manic.) But, there is certainly some basis in believing that a rapid, headlong stroke shows a restless personality.

An outgrowth of the theory that inner being flows through the fingers is the basis for automatic writing, in which an outside control takes over and guides the hand, often voices from the other side. In such a way W. B. Yeats' *A Vision* was dictated to his wife, Georgie. Supposedly the mark of an unstable personality, automatic writing can be psychic and certainly can release inner tension.

Soggy Leaves and Such

Tea leaf fortune telling is simple. Drink your tea. Leave the leaves. The reader tips the cup over. If any tea drips, you are to expect a few tears, but the leaves are there to drive the gloom away. The tea leaf reader is really a story teller and from the residue of leaves can weave a fascinating story about a man with the letter M. Initials and numbers are frequent. The client broods as the fortune teller augurs the symbols. The story is told quickly, for the reader is scurrying in rush hour to her next drinker. Again, money is a chief curse of soggy leaves and tasseography. But also it is one of the most popular practices of tired psychics who live only in fear of the tea bag.

The Danger of Skeleton Keys

I have treated the skeleton keys lightly because so many are absurd to both the Christian and the occultist. Yet there is a danger. A reliance on radiesthesia could keep one from an accredited doctor. If you insist on your dowser, fine; but don't consult him alone. Similarly a dream book may be fun and even revealing, but, if you are disturbed, you need a psychologist not *Soma's Dream Guide*. Opening your Bible at random — holy as the book may be — does not solve the problems your pastor or other professional helpers could.

While most of these keys are disreputable, at least in practice, remember the wonder of a skeleton key is that it opens many doors.

6 KEEPERS OF THE KEYS:

MODERN PSYCHICS

The wonder and danger of all these keys is that humans must unlock the doors. The keys can work for good or bad depending on the keeper. A true keeper needs not only a knowledge of the materials, but that ineffable quality we term the psychic. Its explanation is a puzzle. The voice of the subconscious? Divine inspiration? Discarnate beings? All we know is that this psychic gift is granted to some.

How they use it is another matter. For every saint there is an Aleister Crowley or Sandor de la Vey. There are the confused and the muddled. But each age produces the true devoted psychic. In our age, I think two figures stand above all others: Eileen Garrett, for her parapsychological research, and Edgar Cayce, for his work of healing and enlightening. Both combine the traits of humility and the desire to serve.

I think if we accept the miracles and cures, the predictions and warnings, of the Bible, we can give an ear to these psychics. Both figures are what is termed "trance mediums." I will begin with Mrs. Garrett who not only worked, but defined what she did.

She was born 74 years ago in Ireland, the land of "little people," the leprechauns. As a child she wandered the fields talking to her friends, these little people, whom no one else saw. She was reared by her uncle, who encouraged and accepted her strange powers. Her strange insights caused her to be a troublesome child and, after her uncle's death when Eileen was 15, she was deported to boarding school. But en route she met and married her first husband. With the outbreak of World War I she opened a small cafe, then a hostel to care for the wounded. Her psychic gifts continued. She foresaw the death of her two sons and her second husband.

Many psychic experiences led to a meeting with similarly minded people, and eventually she studied at the College of Psychic Sciences under Hewatt McKenzie, a hard taskmaster, but one who made her psychic powers fully emerge. Without degrees or doctorates, she helped and cured thousands, even a prime minister. She practiced over 50 years to the delight of some, the dismay of many.

Personally she had little time for supernatural bunk as you might discover from her delightful, *The Sense and Nonsense of Prophecy*. Yet holding an envelope, she could tell with frightening detail that it was written by an unhappy girl from New York, the victim of a bad love affair, on a bus to Texas. As mentioned, Mrs. Garrett often worked in a trance, and her controls, disembodied voices, poured forth technical facts, hidden secrets, messages, and information she knew nothing of when awake. In a seance on October 7, 1930, three months after Sir Arthur Conan Doyle's death, she was asked to communicate with him. Instead she began to speak through her control, Uvani, about a dirigible falling and crashing. In more and more technical terms, she told of the tragedy. This was two days after the crash of the British dirigible R-101 in France. When a transcript of the seance was read by the Royal Airship Works, they were astounded. Some even suggested arrest for espionage.

Her biography continues with the names of literary greats, D. H. Lawrence and Aldous Huxley popping up. In 1931, she visited America and throughout the decade pursued an answer to her mediumship and other psychic phenomena. She was in France at the outbreak of World War II. Forced to leave in 1940 for America, she decided to start a publishing house, which she called the Creative Age Press with *Tomorrow* as its literary organ. It attracted such names as Robert Graves, Klaus Mann, Aldous Huxley, and Lord Dunsany. Its first book, *Telepathy,* was by Mrs. Garrett.

Ten years later, in 1951, she established the Parapsychological Foundation in New York to support scientific inquiry, develop an extensive library, hold international conferences, and publish a bi-monthly journal. Mrs. Garrett remained active as a prophet and promoter of parapsychology until her death in 1970.

Always wary of publicity and personal acclaim, Mrs. Garrett believed that everyone has some psychic powers, but that most of us are taught to suppress them. She said, "My investigations of the phenomena of mediumship convince me that these are not extraneous sensitivities, but rather refinements of the physical senses all men possess."

The Sleeping Prophet

An even more unlikely candidate for mediumship and keeper of the keys is Edgar Cayce, born March 18, 1877, in Kentucky. His father was a justice of the peace, his grandfather a dowser, but never was there a psychic in this fundamentalist family (Cayce continued to teach Sunday school all of his life). Edgar and his family received the first clues to his psychic mission at the age of seven when, after reading the story of Samson, he heard a strange, humming sound. A figure in white appeared and said, "Your prayers have been heard. What would you ask of me that I may give it to you?"

Much of Cayce's work concerned health and health readings; the first was for himself when he lost his voice. No one could cure him. While he was under hypnosis, people saw blood rushing to his throat, and the next day Cayce read aloud to them.

In 1902 a phone call changed his life. The school super-intendent's daughter lay dying. Cayce said the trouble was in her spine. It proved true. In spite of his amazing accuracy, his wife, Gertrude, had to convince him time and time again that he was doing right.

His life continued as a series of financial and vocational ups and downs until the 1920s when Cayce and his family moved to Virginia Beach and he began his career of prophecy in earnest. Like Garrett, Cayce was primarily a trance medium but had no controls. Waking or sleeping he was a prophet. Because of the wealth of his predictions, I think we need to break them into categories.

World Prophecies

Cayce disliked these prophecies above all others since he felt they erased free will and the power of prayer. Trying to convince himself that nothing was predestined, only a possibility, he realized that the individual faced with holocaust could exercise little free will in the face of destruction except in the manner in which he accepted it. Thus it might be good to know the future in order to prepare for it.

So he predicted, and I pick not just his hits, but the most familiar examples:

1929   The economic depression.

1935   Union of Austria and Germany, with Japan joining later.

1936   Critical turn from peace (Rhineland, Abyssinia).

1939   The death of two presidents in office.

1941   Russian-German clash. End of the war in 1945.

Health and Cayce

Years before psychosomatic medicine, Cayce with his sixth grade education decided that strains and tensions were the cause of ulcers. It sounds mundane now. Not then. His major premise about health was that there was a cure for everything in nature. Once in his trance state, he diagnosed a case of "a red brain on fire" and prescribed a little known drug which cured the boy. Awake, he could not even pronounce the name of the drug. Another case he diagnosed as pellagra and suggested greens. Doctors had not diagnosed this disease outside of Italy for many years. Long before metal was used in compound fractures, Cayce suggested an iron nail to help a man's life and save his leg from amputation. A most astounding reading occurred when Cayce in mid-trance stopped silent. It was later learned that the man Cayce was reading for, many miles away, had died at the moment Cayce stopped talking.

Cayce was suspicious of doctors and with good reason. During test trances, they had stuck him with pins to attempt to prove he was faking. Deciding to show him as a fake, doctors let a woman they thought needed immediate surgery follow Cayce's diagnosis of an abrasion on the stomach wall and the cure: long walks and a lemon sprinkled with salt. It worked — to the dismay of the doctors.

Cayce eventually worked his cures to simple categories — increased circulation, elimination, assimilation, a proper approach to eating and good exercise. Thus his remedies, too, are simple and direct. To preserve the teeth, he suggested seafood; for anemia, liver. For dread cancer, he predicted a rabbit serum which was later discovered in 1966. He also suggested three almonds a day. Later, chemists found a source for warding off cancer in the almond.

He continued his health readings throughout his life and considered them his major worth. Like all of his readings, they were accomplished under self-induced hypnosis and recorded by a secretary.

Awake and Sleeping

Even when awake Cayce possessed many striking psychic qualities. For example, he saw auras. One day a young woman approached him. He saw a red aura. Cayce said, "Go away and come back when you're not angry." She just came from a quarrel with her husband. Another time he saw no aura around a woman. Two days later she died.

In the dream world, Cayce felt the soul was taking stock of itself and what it had done during the day. Since he believed time was an illusion, dreams could be past, present, or future. An outgrowth of this belief was that almost everything is dreamed before it happens. Although he used dreams and had many pre-cognitive ones himself, he never became a Freudian interpreter and was always bothered by the symbology which varied so much from individual to individual.

You may ask why with dreams and auras and trances, Cayce never made a killing on the stock market or at the race track. Every time he acted selfishly, he became violently ill until he gave up any activity except helping others.

Life Readings

One day in 1923, Cayce went into his usual trance, ready to discuss illness and cures. When he awakened, everyone sat stunned and silent. They reported that he had talked of past lives of the subject. Reincarnation. Cayce was frantic. Surely, this was the work of Anti-Christ. In time, he accepted the belief and gave thousands of life readings with some surprising results. In these readings our Kentucky boy talked in Romance languages, Greek, German, and unknown tongues. He could not pronounce *hors d'oeuvres* awake.

Probing the Past

In 1923 Cayce began to talk of incarnations on Atlantis, the famous sunken continent. Although Plato and 2000 other books existed about Atlantis, Cayce knew nothing of them. Plato and Cayce agreed on much. Cayce said the final breakup of the continent occurred 10,000–12,000 years ago. It occurred in three phases. The first two were around 15,000 B.C. In 10,000 B.C., the last three islands around the Bahamas were swallowed. This was the end of a continent the size of Europe and European Russia. The breakups occurred, Cayce and Plato agreed, because Atlantis was a culture eroded by greed and lust. A few Atlanteans, the Sons of One, escaped to Egypt, Peru, Mexico, Central America, and the North American Southwest.

The sunken continent of Atlantis and its colonizers provide for some the answers to some puzzling questions: Why did calendars of amazing accuracy appear on both sides of the Atlantic at the same time? Why is there a world wide cult of pyramids? Why are there flood stories in every myth cycle? Further evidence is the Piri Reis map drawn long before the Wright brothers, showing Greenland and Antarctica in such detail that only air transport could explain it.

The Future Revealed

Cayce, like many seers, predicts a holocaust in the future. According to Cayce 1958-1998 are crucial years. First, we'll see a change in the physical aspects of the West Coast, probably from earthquakes.

The next stage will see dramatic risings and sinkings in the Mediterranean as a prelude to greater disaster. Further, new land will form in the Atlantic and Pacific. Parts of Japan will slide into the sea. Geologists report that on the Japanese island of Honshu in one volcanic area 87,000 earthquakes occurred in six months during 1965–66.

In America, the Great Lakes will empty into the Gulf of Mexico rather than the St. Lawrence. Geologists attest there is a great crustal break from Missouri to Carolina; the area is tilting and possibly enough for lakes to flow downward to the Mississippi via the Chicago River.

During Cayce's lifetime, 1936 was a crucial year. It witnessed the beginning of the shifting of the earth's axis as well as the political upheavals in Spain, Abyssinia, and the Rhineland. Although nothing visible occurred in 1936, Cayce predicted it would occur first in the earth's core, then spread upward, slowly building pressure and causing the visible shift.

Also, he predicted as a result of the axial tilt, the melting of the ice caps and the inundation of much of the East Coast by water. In 1958, geologists discovered melting caps and that the oceans were rising enough to inundate. Final stages will show great upheavals in the Arctic and torrid zones. Sure enough, a new volcano was found forming over Krakatoa in 1936 and Mt. Irazu in Costa Rica erupted for a year.

The beginning of the end will be manifested by upheavals in the Mediterranean and the Pacific. On schedule, Mt. Etna in Italy erupted more and more in 1964 and a great earthquake occurred in Morocco in 1960. In the Pacific, the earthquakes of Alaska and Japan in the 1960s and the great one in Peru, 1970, were evidence.

Cayce's Beliefs

Cayce's beliefs were simple but pious. He believed that all subconscious minds could communicate, that one could cleanse himself physically and emotionally, and that individuals cured nature.

Psychic wisdom should never be used for material gain. Materialism was a negative force defeating a God-given purpose. He accepted karma and its purpose. He attributed long life to selflessness. And he was a breaker of all barriers between religions crossing Christianity, Judaism, Hinduism, and Buddhism. Most important, he believed that man's misuse of natural forces was the cause of the first catastrophe and that going against divine law continues to affect nature.

Whether he was a saint or a syncretist, one cannot impugn Cayce's motives, deny his results, nor curse his life. In fact, he was so devoted to helping that he wore himself out. During World War II, he gave so many health and life readings that he became a broken man, dying January 3, 1946, of exhaustion and natural kindness.

The Test of the Prophet

So the years spin. Each age produces its seer or prophet. It would be and often is the occultist's delight to write in exclamation marks. And then this came true!!! But the final test of a psychic is not his accuracy. A prophet like Aleister Crowley at the turn of the century and into the 1940's predicted through high sexual magic. Nor is the test mysticism. Madame Blavatsky, the founder of the Theosophists, remains shrouded in tangled repute because of her reliance on mystery. Perhaps the test is honesty and reverence, a blend of will and selflessness that does not turn to the exclamation point but to the question mark: why was I granted this power?

7   A FUTURE DOOR?

As we sit waiting for the apocalypse, for the world to execute its final bump and grind, a frantic search spreads. The searchers are primarily the young or the disenchanted. A new age bookshelf might well contain the *I Ching* and the sayings of Chairman Mao, *The Politics of Experience* and *The Sacred Tarot*. In a rejection of traditional western values, revolution and religion couple. The child is Religious Revolution or Revolutionary Religion.

If some eternal ledger keeper weighs the arcane antics of the decade, he will find a suit as mottled as a jester's. It will contain the old maidish ladies of high moral unctuousness and smelling of dead roses who carefully shuffle their cards and buy cat horoscopes. It will contain the Sunday gnostic who thinks astrology is "Wow! A freaky trip." It will contain Mansons and Zodiac killers. Young people in America, land of the free, home of the melting pot, have melted the occult, welded on revolution, and tossed out the church, Dupont, and General Westmoreland with one sweep of the witches' Molotov broom.

This new trip is radical for many young people. It is crucial. It is involved. It contains none of the sardonic attachment of the past. You're in or out. The occult's in; revolution's in. The church is out; government is out. Why?

The Quest for Mystery

When the West poured forth its grail and it contained a mushroom cloud, a generation began — a generation without a future or, at least, with the gnawing notion that a future did not necessarily exist. Replies that science and technology gave us not just the mushroom cloud but dishwashers to clean the mushroom stains do not suffice.

Nor will mutterings that if the material world has lost its appeal, why not go to church? Many of the young feel that the church married Mammon over the collection plate and they resent its slapdash red thermometer showing the contribution goal for the year jutting phallically between the font and the cross. Maybe they've sat through Sunday school and the very word "school" devaluates it for the young. Why not Sun Day? Maybe they've been told that Christianity is believable, is historical, is right, is factual, is sound, is logical, is reasonable.

And maybe they've choked on believability and fact. You don't need logic in an apocalypse. The church has glutted them with fact. The disenchanted want mystery, not miracles explained. They want the divine nonsense of God incarnated in the flesh. And the quest for the historical Jesus has led them from the font into a wasteland.

Outside the church mysteries abound. Whether it is the shuffling of the Tarot, the tossing of the *I Ching,* the deciphering of names, there is mystery and myth. The occult speaks the language of myth and sings the language of myth and wraps itself in the red draperies of myth. But myth is not fairy tale. I agree with Ananda Coomaraswamy, who says myth is the highest expression of truth. Why? Myth may be lost in history, something we recall only in the dim recesses of our mind or leftovers of ancient events. Mythic language tells stories, and this language binds the loosely skeined threads of logic and knowledge into a story that expresses psychic truth, if not physical fact. These stories grasp intuitively what reason cannot.

Myth is highest truth, for it expresses in concrete terms what reason merely fumbles and drops. The factual language of abstract science or history cannot absorb the real truths of religion because they analyze rather than integrate experience. Religion and occultism are intuitive, psychic, mythic. When either strays into abstraction and analysis, danger lies ahead.

The Quest for Celebration

Too often the church gives the young an organ with emphysema, an off-key choir, and a soprano who sings all hymns louder than the congregation. Many are moved to madness by the dull and dusty rituals, codified and rigidified, and ossified through centuries. The young see this fumbling Sunday ritual and reject it.

It is celebration they want, even play in its highest sense. Celebration is based on community, signified by the kiss of peace in ancient Christian rites. Celebration is based on hope. The church tries, oh, it tries to celebrate, but it suffers a cosmic disease of failed imagination. Maybe the southern Alleluia shouters are as close to celebration as the church comes. More important, many cannot celebrate because they have no "God-consciousness-within," those mysterious words of the occult. The occult, like it or not, is imaginative and creative, is even a cause for celebration as the alienated individual finds the God within. Playful is a word for the children of the apocalypse, complete with the divine fool of the Tarot dressed as hippie court jester and handing flowers while humming "Om."

The enemy of celebration and play is reason. No wonder astrology flourishes as the beginner's art. It begins in the inescapable reason of mathematics and ends in cosmic irrationality. Maybe the Tarot, the *I Ching,* and numerology combine irrationality with hope, a hope for answers, a hope that the grail will be alchemized to an elixir of ecstasy and mystery.

With the rejection of reason, with the idea that reason fails, the young need hope, for it is fearful to be lost in the lonely crowd with no props. And the occult offers props, hope, even salvation, a union beyond the apocalypse. Its very value may lie in the fact that reason gives way to flowers, science to Tarot, moon shots to astrology. It is an answer. It does contain the elements of celebration. It is irrational in the best sense. And it offers eternity.

The Quest for Community

The church calls to salvation, and it calls in such a way that many feel guilt, and guilt spurs one on or turns one off. The occult insists not so much for a striving out of guilt as for a liberation of inner resources, psychic energy, communion of minds. It is exactly this sense of liberation that leads students to the occult. The with-in-ness, the at-one-ness, answer a need crying and unheard, they feel, by the church. The practice of the occult usually involves others. Its followers find community, sharing, and yes, even love for one another. The church also claims to provide this, but many young people do not find community there.

The church needs to look seriously at this desire for community. If community is lost, the church is lost. For the church is the mystical body of Christ; let Christians rediscover this meaning. Behind the drug communes and the hypnotic eroticism of Charles Manson is the search for a leader and a home. For the sake of the young, hope that the leader is a St. Francis and not a Manson. Pray the community is a church and not a coven.

The Occult and Christianity

Between the spirit of the occult and its content falls the irreparable breach between Christianity and the occult. Its God is

not the Christian God and cannot be. No matter how hard occultists strain to show Christ as theirs, to show that the mystic
was deleted from the Gospels, he is not their sole savior. He is
not, for occultists, the son of God. The breach widens when the
occultist's goal is not to be like God, to emulate him, but to
become God. No matter how devout this heresy or the purity of
its intent, it does not recognize the insurmountable gulf between
man and God that can be spanned only by God coming in Christ
to build the bridge. The occult does not acknowledge the biblical view that man lacks the strength to climb the ladder and become part of the Godhead. The corollary belief in reincarnation
and karma is another impossible leap for a Christian. Christ's
atonement and resurrection offer the only hope for the future;
sin makes human perfection impossible.

Indeed, it would be petty to think the world bends to
our will, that incantations and pentagrams and hexes and oracles
will bring us the golden apples of the sun, the green desires of
Washington bills. All would like wealth and splendor and fame.
And it would be pretty to sight through burnt-out afternoons that
fate was splotched on a circle called a horoscope or a spread
of cards. This is too easy. A Christian bends to God's will, he
does not bend God's will to his. And the tree of life does not
bend branches to us. We picked the fruit and lost the tree pre-
cisely because we did not bend to God's will. I am not saying
the occult is merely for selfish ends, certainly not fatalistic ones,
but the temptation to both is there and too few can resist it.

Similarly, I would like the comfort of a dualistic universe
where like halves of an apple, good and evil are separate but
equal. But what of the core? We cannot escape it. God is one.
Evil is man's realm; good is God's. God is above and surrounding
and strengthening, but he is not part of the eternal pull, the strug-
gle to unite opposites. He is not the halves, but the core.

In this breach between beliefs, I avoid as much as possible biblical injunctions against the occult; not because they frighten me but because they've been worked to death and I think they are answered. The Witch of Endor was consulted by Saul because he lacked the patience to find God revealing himself in history. The astrologers of Pharaoh and Nebuchadnezzar failed because they augured the fate not the character of mankind and found the futility of their gods, not the hope of the Hebrew God.

In brief, it means the occult cannot replace God or become God, that fate is in ourselves and with God. Man cannot and should not know his fate. The occult is not totally dangerous, but it is not a plaything or a bauble.

Yet I fear you may reject all of the occult as nothing more than a frivolous fad. I fear because mystery is so unpopular in an age of logic and reason. And I fear because even a true believer in the occult may believe in the wrong things.

Yet I have hope. Hope that people within and without the church may look beyond the fads and frauds of the occult to see the spiritual hunger that drives young and old to search for wisdom and experience in the occult world.

I have hope.

Hope that the church can rediscover elements of its tradition that have been lost in the morass of intellectualizing and organizing.

Hope that the church can rise above its concern with buildings and programs to offer again a real sense of community.

Hope that the church can stop trying to explain away the mysteries of the faith to appeal to the skeptical and positivistic modern mind.

Hope that we can again revel in the mysticism and ecstasy of the early church.

Hope that we can again learn to celebrate the goodness of a loving God who frees us from the shackles of fate by the life and death and resurrection of Christ.

Hope that by faith in a Holy Fool we can all find the peace which passes understanding.

145270

FURTHER READINGS IN THE OCCULT

Since an interest in the occult can become expensive, I have listed books which I have found most useful and least expensive.

General Works on the Occult

Cavendish, Richard. *The Black Arts.* New York: G. P. Putnam Sons, Capricorn Paperback, 1968.
The title implies a certain bias against the occult, but behind the skepticism is a good overview of numerology, alchemy, astrology, the Tarot, and Satanism.

Christian, Paul. *History and Practice of Magic.* New York: Citadel Press, 1969.
An expensive but monumental work by a 19th century occultist, covering beliefs, practices, and most branches of the occult.

Crow, W. B. *Witchcraft, Magic, and Occultism.* Alhambra, Calif.: Borden Publishing Co., 1968.
A rather cursory search through the history of the occult, but valuable for its historical perspective.

Gibson, Walter B. and Litzkar. *The Complete Illustrated Book of the Psychic Sciences.* New York: Simon and Schuster, Pocket Books, 1968.
More of a grab bag than a complete or scientific study, but it deals with every possible topic from aeromancy to mole-osophy. Amusing for those who enjoy the skeleton keys or need a quick reference for minor information.

Beliefs and Practices

Hunt, Douglas. *Exploring the Occult*. New York: Ballantine Books, 1964.
A brief compendium of beliefs useful for the novice.

Rampa, Lobsang. *You, Forever*. New York: Dell Publishing Co., 1965.
Interesting reading, but too stridently demanding reincarnation to be totally acceptable.

Stevenson, Ian. *Twenty Cases Suggestive of Reincarnation*. New York: American Society for Psychical Research, 1966.
Surely the most authoritative, least presumptuous, book on reincarnation.

Steiger, Brad, and Williams, Loring. *Other Lives*. New York: Hawthorn Books, 1969.
Nice reading, but too superficial a view of reincarnation. Best on suggested cases.

Watts, Alan. *The Two Hands of God*. New York: Macmillan Co., Collier Books, 1969.
The most fascinating probing look at dualism I have encountered.

Astrology

Davison, Ronald. *Astrology*. New York: Arco Publishing Co., 1963.
The best and simplest book for the beginner. Deals with theory and practice.

Goodavage, Joseph. *Astrology: The Space Age Science*. New York: New American Library, Signet Books, 1966.
A noble attempt to make astrology more scientific, valuable in recounting theory and provoking thought.

MacNeice, Louis. *Astrology*. New York: Doubleday and Co., 1964.
That rare combination — a beautifully written yet reliable history, theory, and practice of astrology. Expensive, but worth it.

Rudhyar, Dane. *The Astrology of Personality*. New York: Doubleday and Co., 1970.
A provocative and extensive work, but not for the reader with only passing interest.

—————. *The Practice of Astrology*. Baltimore, Md.: Penguin Books, 1968.
A good step-by-step look at astrology, which includes the ethics of astrology as well as the practice.

The Tarot

Doane, Doris C. and Keyes, King. *How to Read Tarot Cards*. New York: Funk and Wagnalls Paperback, 1967.
A purely divinatory work listing meanings. Useful if you can relate symbols to the listings, otherwise a mere pawn for fortune tellers.

Heline, Corrine. *The Bible and the Tarot*. Oceanside, Calif.; New Age Press, 1969.
An attempt to relate the two, but it is quite a strain. The author is best when dealing with the meaning of symbols.

Papus. *The Tarot of the Bohemians*. Alhambra, Calif.: Borden Publishing Co., 1971.
A rather involved, but popular text, heavy on divination.

The Tarot Revealed. New York: New American Library, Signet Book.

Almost entirely divinatory, but gives some emphasis to the meaning of symbols.

Waite, A. E. *A Pictorial Key to the Tarot.* New Hyde Park, N.Y.: University Book, Inc., 1959.

Quite reliable, but rather dependent on the author's idiosyncratic theories.

Numerology

Cheiro's Book of Numbers. New York: Arco Publishing Co., 1964.

About as authoritative as one gets in numerology.

Goodman, Morris. *Modern Numerology.* New York: Fleet Press, 1945.

Well-written, but considers only the modern system.

Lopez, Vincent. *Numerology: How to Be Your Own Numerologist.* New York: New American Library, Signet Books, 1961.

A very pop version of numbers. Interesting on the meaning of numbers, weak on history and practice.

Divinations and Prophecy

Garrett, Eileen, *The Sense and Nonsense of Prophecy.* New York: Berkely Medallion Book, 1968.

A delightful account of much of the chaff of occultism: tea leaves, crystal balls, palmistry, and the like.

Gettings, Fred. *The Book of the Hand*. Prague: Hamlyn Publishing Group, 1968.

Removes the dross from palmistry and shows its historical significance.

Leek, Sybil. *Sybil Leek's Book of Fortune Telling*. New York: Macmillan, 1969.

The jet set occultist's usual slapdash of tea leaves, candle wax, and crystal balls; amounts to little except amusing reading.

Legge, James, tr. *I Ching*. New York: Bantam Books, 1969.

A rather weighty tome, but worth it if you are interested in this Oriental practice.

Psychics and Mediums

Bro. Harmon. *Edgar Cayce on Religion and Psychic Experience*. New York: Paperback Library, 1970.

Rather turgid reading, but valuable for the Christian interested in the occult.

Garrett, Eileen. *Many Voices*. New York: Dell Publishing Co., 1968.

Garrett's own fascinating biography of her life as a medium.

Pike, James. *The Other Side*. New York: Dell Publishing Co., 1968.

A fascinating account of one theologian's encounter with the occult.

Rohmer, Sax. *The Romance of Sorcery*. New York: Paperback Library, 1970.

Rather cursory, but a good introduction to the lives of famous psychics.

Stearn, Jess. *Edgar Cayce: The Sleeping Prophet*. New York: Doubleday.

The very readable biography that made America Cayce-conscious.